Dedicated to all those who have lost hope. May you be blessed with Love, A Safe Space, and Peace. May your brokenness be healed, and wholeness restored.

I came from a system that failed me.

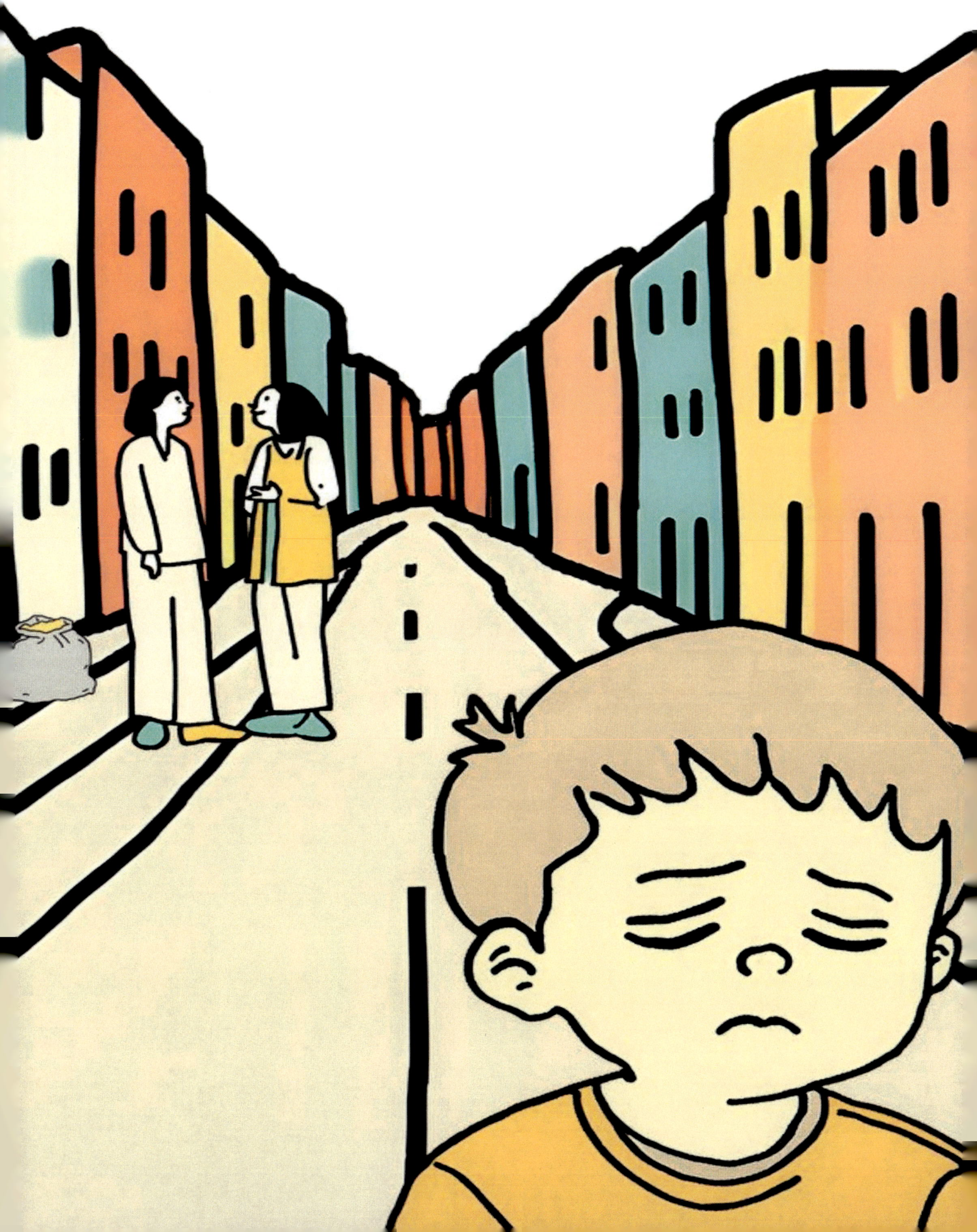

Hurt and abused with no sign of hope. The pain I bear is far too great and now I am in a system filled with unfamiliar faces.

Child Protective Services

Strangers tell me that they will love and care for me, but don't they know those words mean nothing to me.

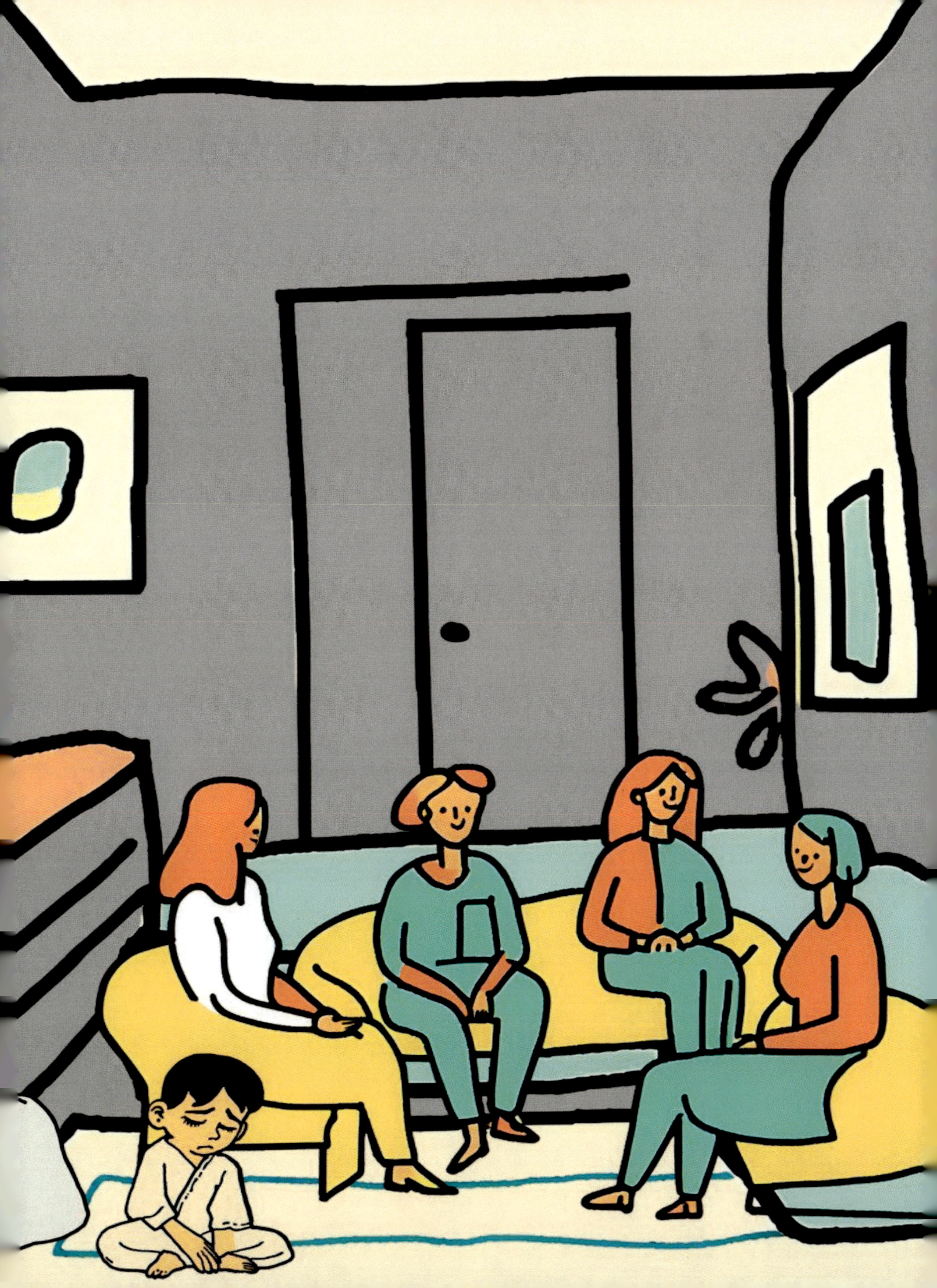

They don't even know me, so how can they love me.

We love you

All I want to do is hide, hide my scars, hide my pain, hide my neglect, hide my trauma, just simply disappear.

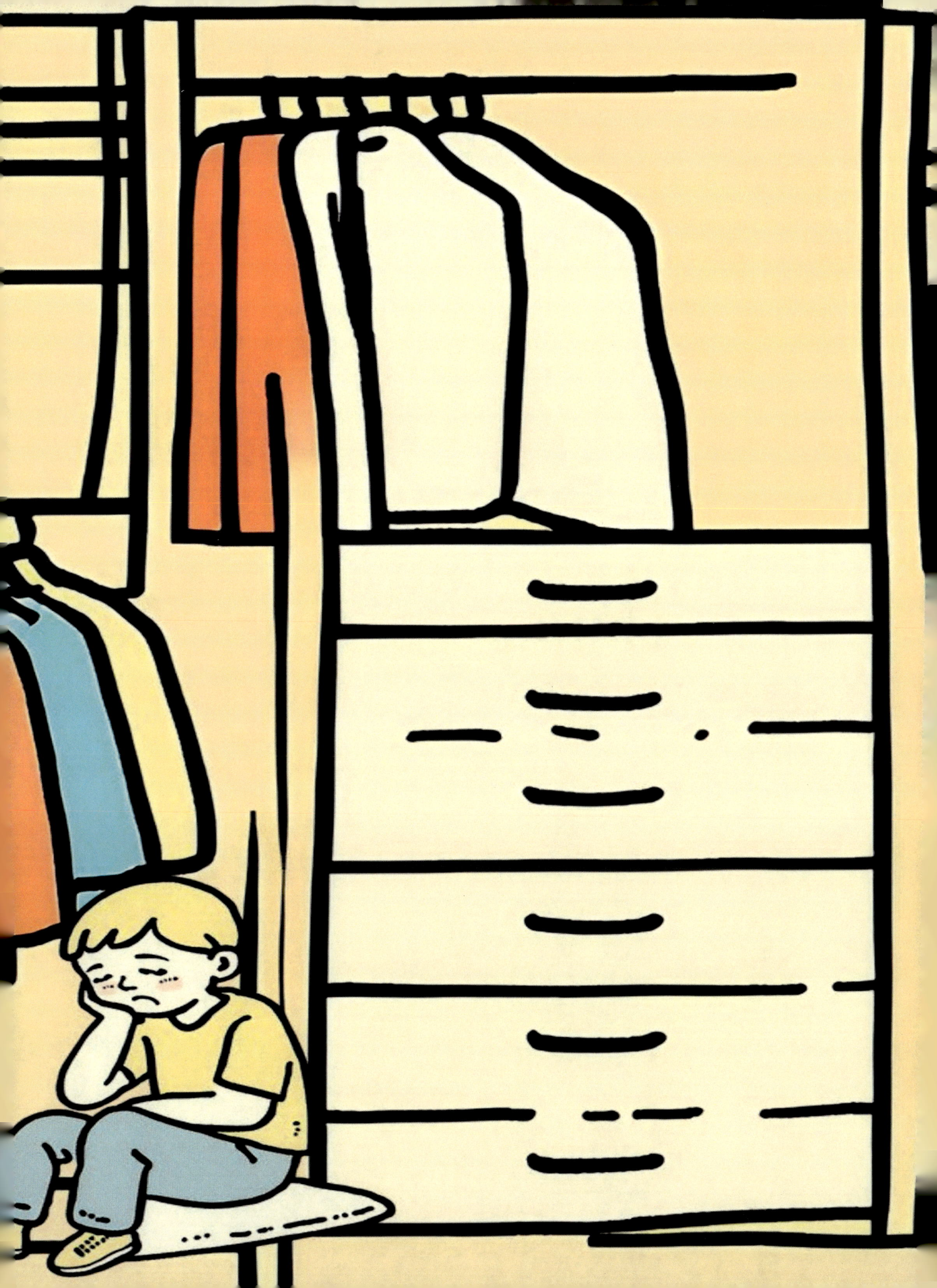

If they can't find me then they can't hurt me.

"I feel alone"
"no one loves me"
"Everything is my fault"
"I want to go home"

But they look at me and smile, my face remains emotionless. Yet every day they continue to smile.

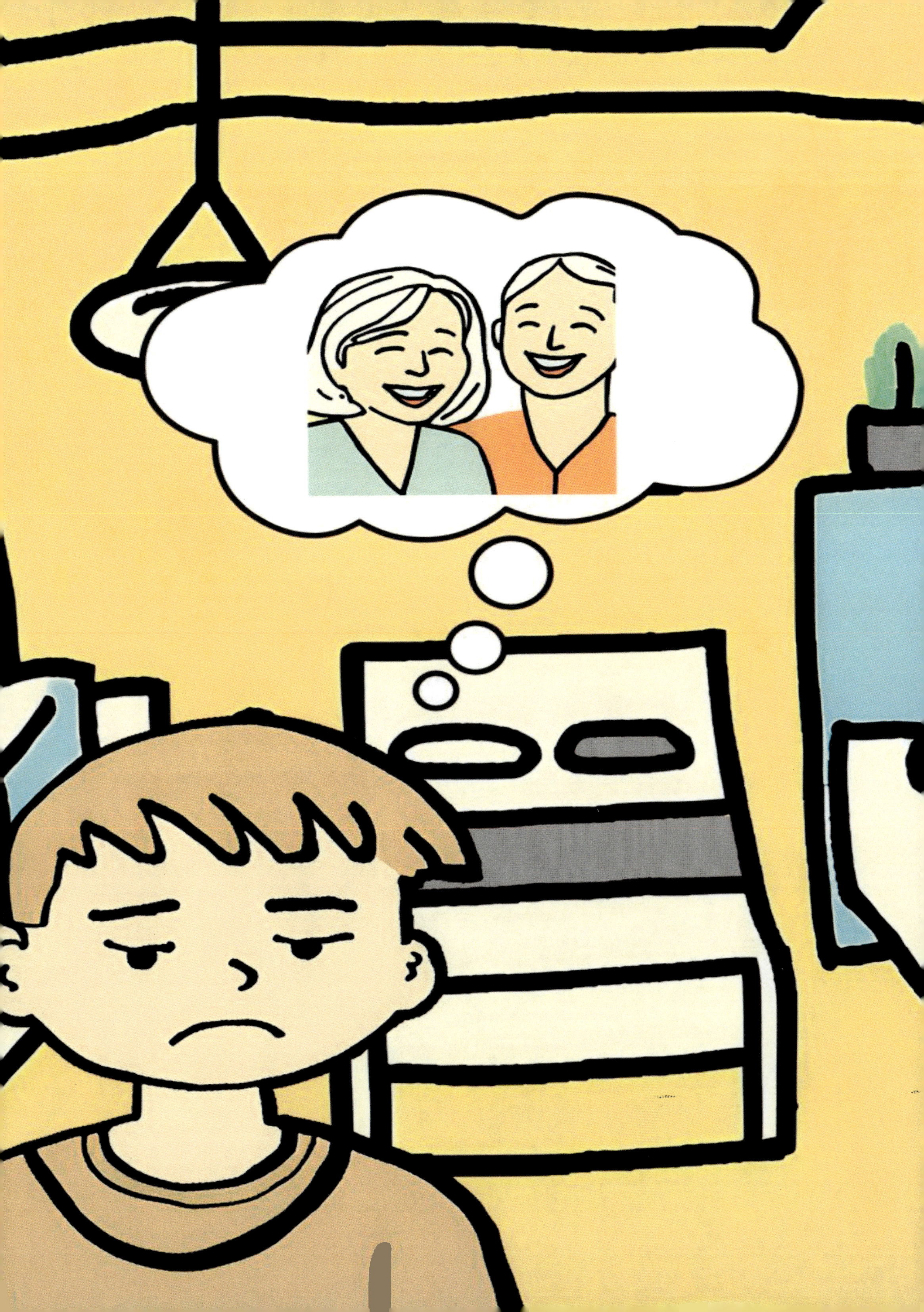

Days in and days out, this one continues to smile. No matter how I try to sabotage, they continue to try.

"Everything will be ok...would you like to talk about it"

They feed and clothed me, wow I have clean clothes and food to eat. A comfortable bed in a clean home, this must be a trick.

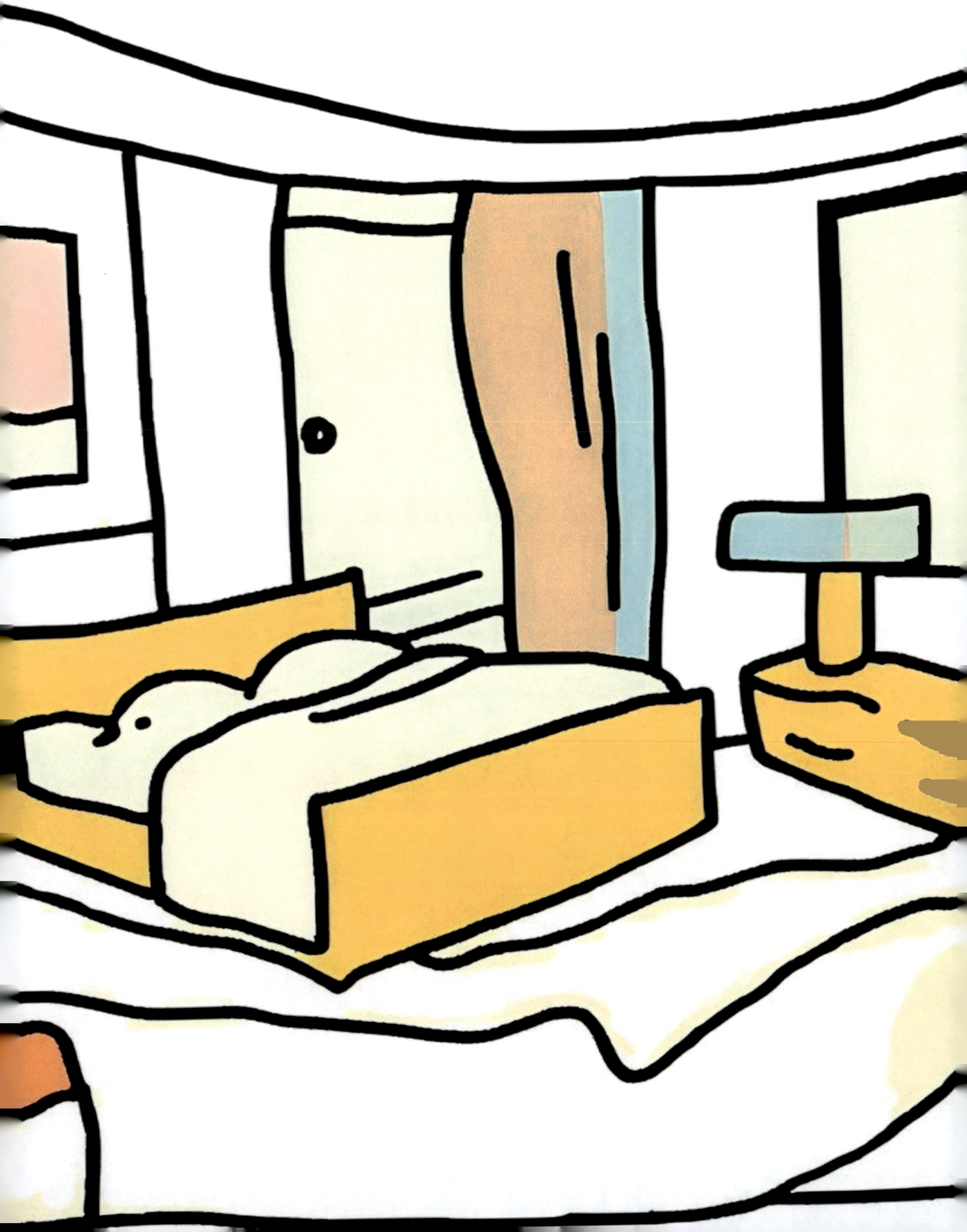

I steal and hide all I can because I feel this will not last.

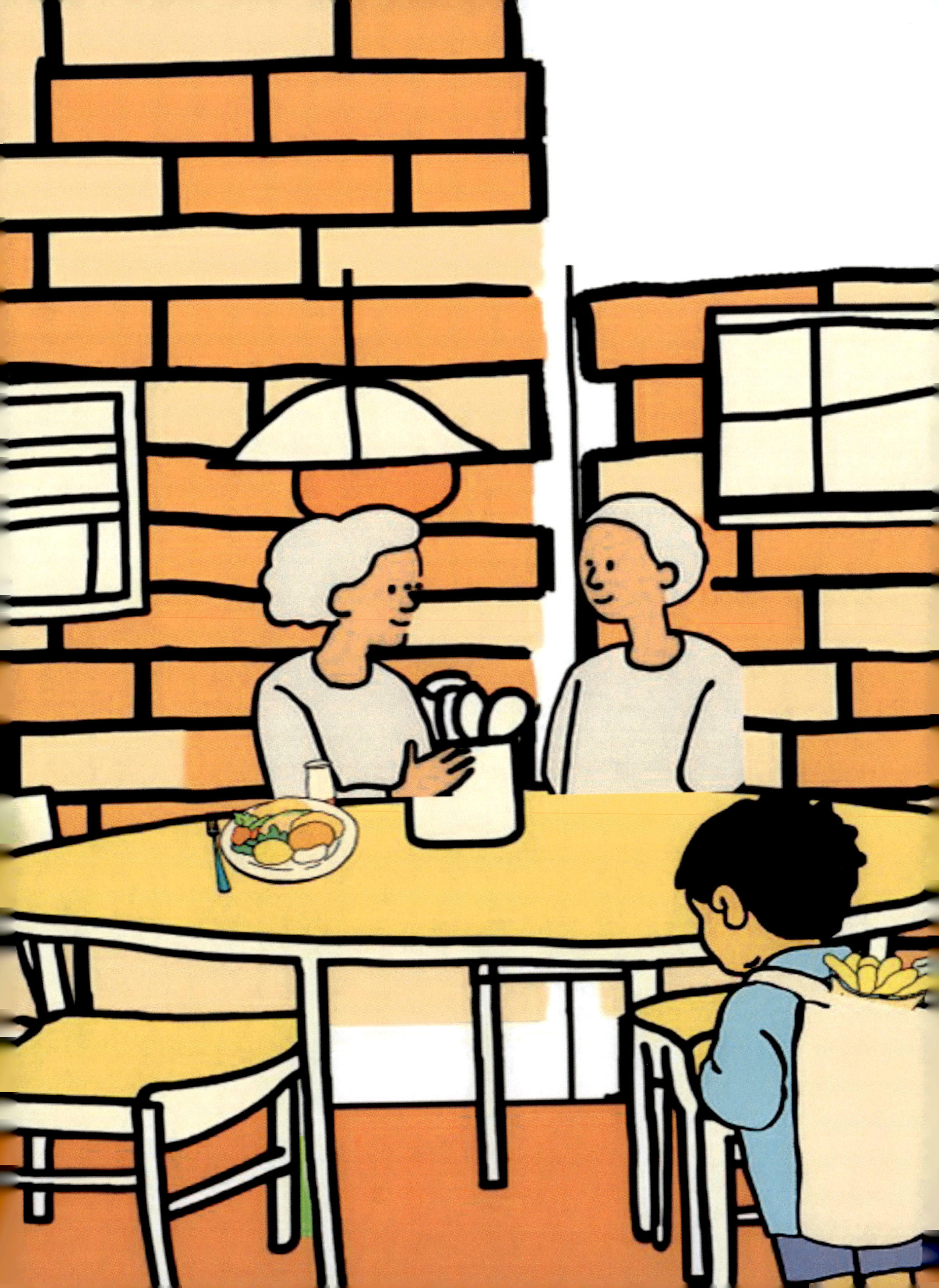

Their true colors will come out wait and see.

Yet...

Every day they greet me with a warm welcome. Every day they tell me God is good. Consistently the same every day, I wonder why they are choosing to keep me.

"welcome home"

Then they tell me, I am loved. Something about God loves me, they love me and that I am blessed. They say I am good; I am smart, I am funny, and I can be anything I want to be.

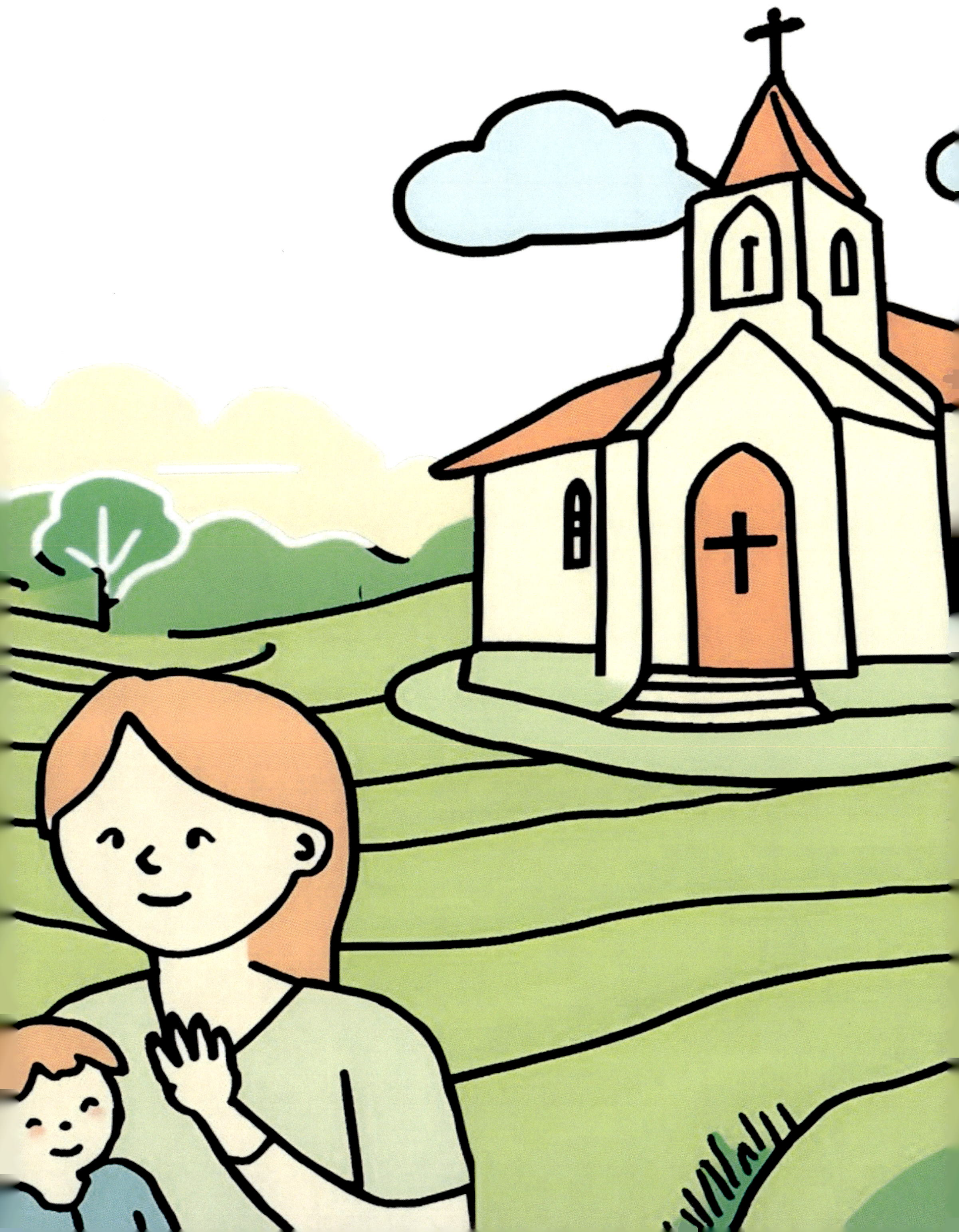

I hear this so much, then suddenly one day my pain and sorrows start to fade.

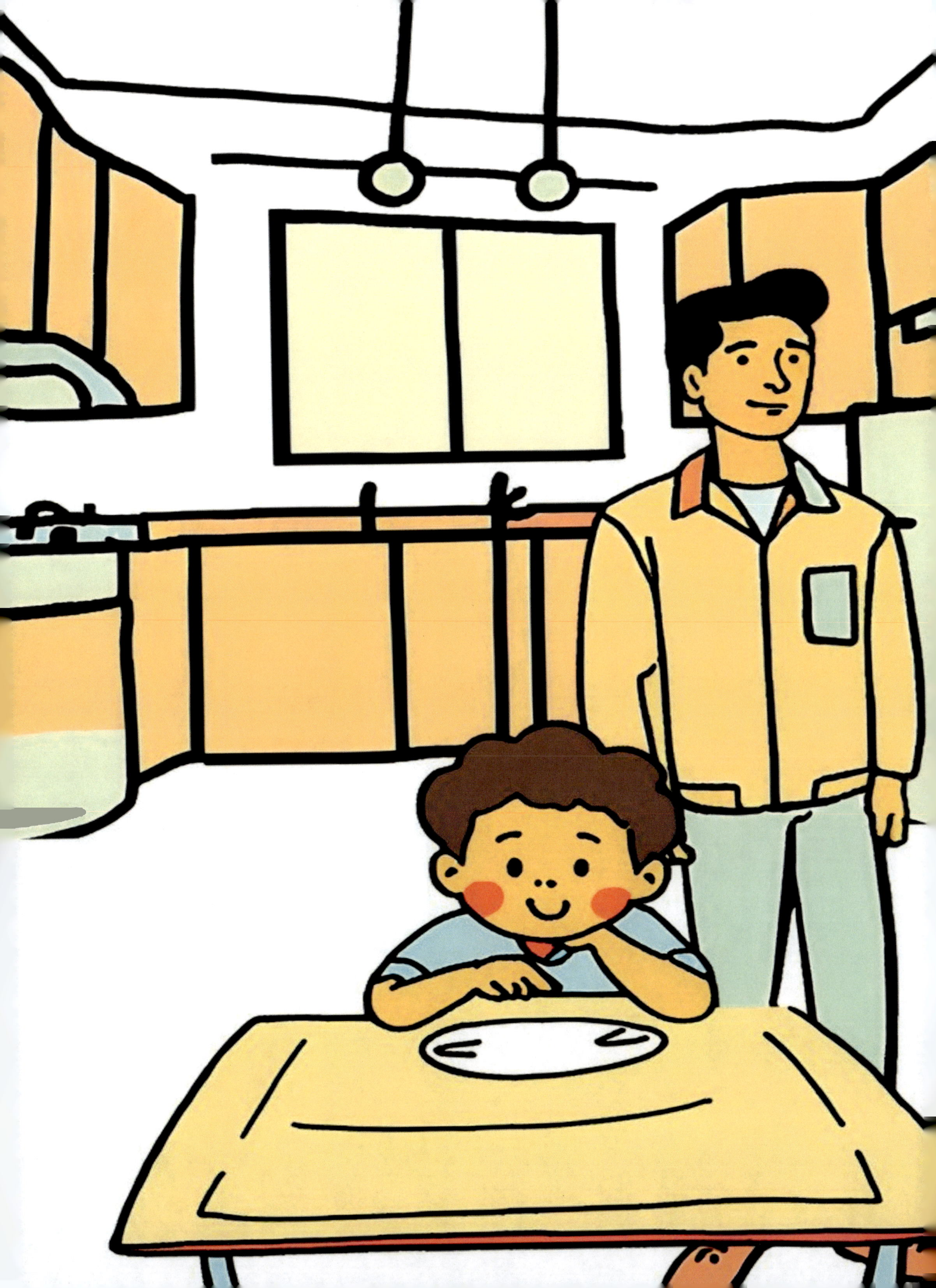

I never thought this existed, being in a place where I could be safe. I no longer want to hide. I have Hope that each day will be better than the one before.

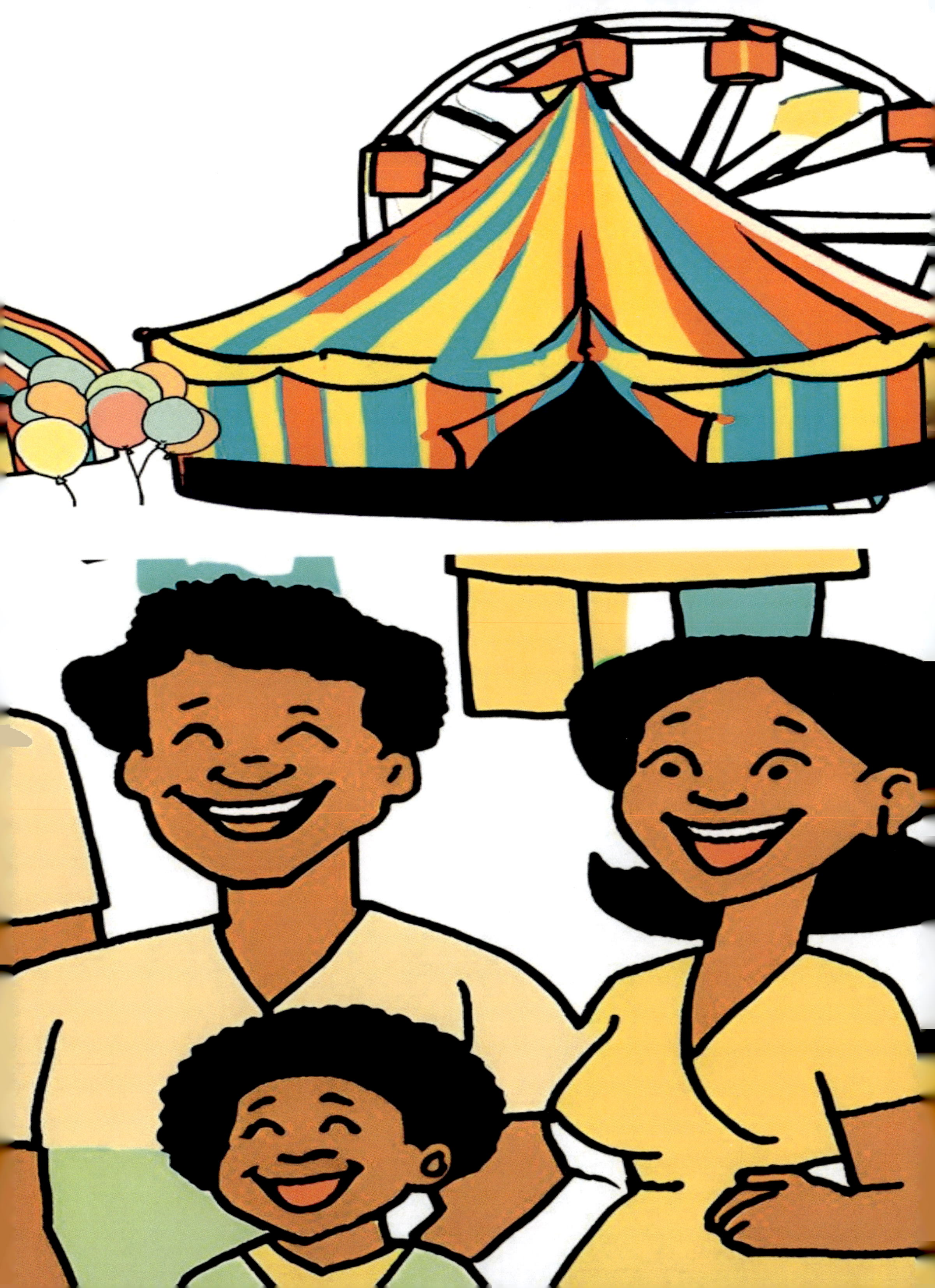

Made in the USA
Middletown, DE
17 September 2024